A House Built Uneven:

Race, Power, and the American Church

A Narrative for
Seven Rhythms of Racial Healing and
Reconciliation in God's Church

Title

A House Built Uneven: Race, Power, and the American Church

Author: Dirrick Williams

First Edition Publication Year 2026

Permissions

For permissions, speaking engagements, or bulk distribution inquiries, contact: dirrick@dirrickwilliams.com

ISBN: 979-8-9946274-5-7

Copyright Page

This manuscript is intended for educational, faith-based, and personal development purposes. While every effort has been made to ensure the accuracy of the information contained herein, the author assumes no responsibility for errors or omissions, or for damages resulting from the use of the information contained in this work

Statement of Intent

This work is written as an invitation into truth, reflection, and transformation. It is not intended to condemn, but to clarify; not to divide, but to reveal what must be addressed in order for genuine reconciliation to occur within the Christian church.

Dedicated to my wife, Joy. Whose support, patience, and understanding are the marvel of my life.

Table of Contents

Introduction:

Why This Work Cannot Be Avoided

The cost of silence, the value of truth

There is a moment that comes in every difficult conversation. It doesn't always arrive at the beginning. Often, it emerges quietly, somewhere in the middle—after the history has been named, after the patterns have been described, after the tension has begun to settle into the room.

 It is not always spoken out loud, but it is felt. It is the question beneath all other questions:

Why does this matter?

- Why does this need to be done?
- Why revisit what is painful?
- Why disrupt what feels stable?

- Why press into something that many have learned to live around, rather than through?

For some, the question is genuine. For others, it is protective. For many, it is both. Because if the answer is not clear, if the value is not understood, then the work will always feel optional. And anything that feels optional will eventually be avoided.

So, this must be said plainly. This work matters because what has been left unaddressed has not remained neutral. It has continued.

Silence does not preserve peace. It preserves patterns. And the patterns that have shaped the American church, those formed in unequal systems, sustained through normalized structures, and carried forward through unexamined assumptions—are still shaping it today.

To ignore them is not to escape them. It is to participate in them.

For many people, faith has been understood as something deeply personal.

- A relationship with God.
- A journey of belief.
- A commitment to growth.

And all of that is true. But what is often left unexamined is how that personal faith has been formed. Not just by scripture, but by environment. By culture. By what has been taught, modeled, and normalized.

A person may believe they have independently arrived at their understanding of faith, but the truth is no one is formed in isolation.

Every sermon heard, every leader followed, every church experience encountered.

All of it shapes how faith is understood. And if those environments were shaped by imbalance, then that formation carries that imprint.

This does not make someone guilty. But it does make them responsible. They are not responsible for what they inherited. But for what they do with it.

Because unexamined formation limits growth. It creates blind spots. Not intentional ones, but real ones.

- Blind spots in how others are understood.
- Blind spots in how justice is interpreted.
- Blind spots in how the gospel is lived out in relationship to the world.

And those blind spots have consequences.

They shape how people respond to pain they have not experienced. They influence how they interpret stories that challenge their assumptions. They determine whether they listen—or dismiss.

This work matters because it removes those blind spots. Not all at once, but progressively. It allows a person to see more clearly. To understand more fully. To engage more honestly.

And that is not a loss of faith, it is a deepening of it. Because faith that cannot withstand truth is not faith. It is fragility, and fragility cannot sustain transformation.

Why This Matters to Community

The church is not only a collection of individuals. It is a body, and a body cannot function fully if parts of it are unseen, unheard, or undervalued.

The language of unity has long been central to the church. But unity without honesty is not unity; it is uniformity. And uniformity requires silence. It requires that differences be minimized and that tensions be avoided. That discomfort should be suppressed. And we all know that suppressed tension does not disappear. It accumulates.

It shows up in who speaks—and who does not. In who leads—and who is overlooked. In whose experiences are centered—and whose are sidelined.

A community may appear peaceful. But that peace may come at the cost of truth. And peace that requires silence is not peace.

This work matters because it restores integrity to the community. It creates space for honesty, difference, and tension that leads to growth rather than division. It allows people to bring their full selves, not just the parts that fit. And when that happens, we experience a shift.

- Trust deepens.
- Relationships strengthen.
- Understanding expands.

Because a real community is not built on avoidance, it is built on engagement.

Why This Matters to the Church

At its core, the church is called to embody something, not just to teach it. Not just to proclaim it, but to live it. A message of reconciliation, of unity, of justice and love.

But a message that is not reflected in practice loses credibility. Not immediately, but gradually. And as the message continues while the practice lacks, people see and feel the gap between what is said and what is lived.

Over time, that gap creates distance, especially for those who have experienced the weight of that inconsistency most directly.

- Younger generations notice it.
- Communities of color feel it.
- Those outside the church observe it.

And the result is not always rejection, but sometimes quiet disengagement.

- A stepping back.
- A loss of trust.
- A question that lingers:
  Does the church believe what it says?

This work matters because it addresses that question. Not through explanation, but through alignment. Alignment between belief and structure, between message and practice, between intention and reality.

Because the church's credibility is not determined by its doctrine alone, it is determined by its embodiment. And embodiment requires change - not surface change, but structural change. The kind of change that reshapes how leadership is formed, how decisions are made, and how voices are included.

The kind of change that moves beyond diversity to equity. Beyond inclusion to shared authority. Beyond proximity to transformation.

The Cost of Not Doing This Work

It is important to name this clearly, because avoiding this work does not preserve the church; it weakens it.

It creates a version of faith that is disconnected from reality. A version of community that cannot sustain honesty. A version of leadership that reflects history more than calling. And over time, that disconnection becomes visible through:

- Declining trust.
- Disengaged members.
- Communities that feel unseen, and
- leaders who struggle to respond to the moment they are in.

The Value of Doing This Work

And yet, this is not only about cost, but also about possibility. Because when the church engages this work honestly, something becomes available that was not accessible before.

- Clarity
- Depth
- Integrity

Elements of relationship emanating from a faith that is not fragile, but resilient. A community that is not performative—but real. A church that does not avoid tension—but grows through it.

Church then becomes a place where reconciliation is not spoken of as an idea but experienced as a practice: not perfect, but present.

And that kind of church carries weight, not because it has solved everything, but because it has chosen truth over comfort. And truth has always been the foundation of transformation.

The Question That Remains

So, the question is not whether this work is difficult; we know it is. The question is not whether it will create tension; we know it will. The question is not whether it will cost something; we know it does. The question is this: **Is the cost of avoidance greater than the cost of engagement?**

Because one leads to preservation of what is already uneven, and the other leads slowly, imperfectly, but genuinely to transformation.

And transformation is what the church
was always meant to embody.

Final Chapter, first:

When it's hard, it is an Invitation to continue anyway.

There is something important to say before you move forward. And that is, this work is not easy.

Not because it is unclear. Not because it is unnecessary. But because it is **deeply human**.

As you engage this journey—through reading, reflecting, listening, and honestly examining your own formation, you may notice things rising within you that you did not expect.

You may feel:
Hesitation — a quiet resistance to going further.

- ➤ **Discomfort** — a sense that something is being unsettled.

- ➤ **Confusion** — not knowing exactly what to do with what you are learning.

- ➤ **Defensiveness** — an instinct to protect what has always felt normal.

- ➤ **Guilt or Shame** — even when no accusation has been made.

- ➤ **Fatigue** — emotional or mental weariness.

- ➤ **Fear** — of saying the wrong thing, thinking the wrong thing, or being misunderstood.

And for some, there may be something deeper:

> **Latent pain** - connected to personal or collective experiences.

> **Unresolved wounds** - that have never been given space.

> **Memories or realities** - that have long been avoided or minimized

If any of this happens, you should know that although you may experience these or similar thoughts and feelings, contrary to how you may interpret your immersion, you are not failing. Rather, you feel and experience these thoughts and emotions because you are actively engaging... and that's a good thing.

This work is challenging because it touches on personal identity and asks questions like:

> "How did I come to see the world this way?"

> ➢ "What have I inherited?"
> ➢ "What has shaped me without my awareness?"

These are not surface-level questions. They move beneath opinions, assumptions, and habits and into the deeper places where beliefs are formed, experiences are stored, and meaning is developed.

When those places are engaged, it can feel unsettling. Not because something is wrong—but because something is being revealed.

There is no requirement to process everything at once. There is no expectation that you will:

> ➢ Understand everything immediately
> ➢ Resolve every tension
> ➢ Respond perfectly

This is not a test; this is a journey. You are allowed to:

> Pause

> Reflect

> Ask questions

> Sit with uncertainty

Growth that is rushed rarely lasts. Growth that is honest and steady tends to live much longer. And for that reason, we believe and live that Safety Matters.

This work was never intended to be done in a way that overwhelms or isolates you. In fact, your emotional, spiritual, and relational safety has been considered throughout the design of this process.

That is why this journey includes:

> Gradual progression (not abrupt confrontation)

> Space for reflection (not constant pressure)

> Guided practices (not unstructured exposure)

> ➤ Communal engagement (not isolation)

You are not being asked to carry this alone, nor pushed beyond what can be held with care. However, safety does not mean the absence of discomfort.

It means:

> ➤ You are not being attacked
> ➤ You are not being rushed
> ➤ You are not being required to perform

It means you have space to:

> ➤ Think honestly
> ➤ Feel deeply
> ➤ Grow gradually

Safety is not about avoiding the work; it's about engaging in a way that allows you to stay present within it. At some point, you may feel the desire to disengage. To say:

> ➤ "This is too much."

- ➢ "This is not for me."
- ➢ "I don't need to go any further."

And that moment is important. It is a critical moment, and as practitioners, it is a moment longed for and greatly respected. Because often, that is not where the work ends, but where it begins to matter most.

It is an invitation to gently ask:

- ➢ "What is this feeling trying to protect?"
- ➢ "What might I discover if I stay just a little longer?"

When you arrive at this point, it is reassuring to know others are walking this path with you. Some may be ahead of you, some beside you, and some just beginning. But the truth is, there is no perfect place to be, but the awareness of others being here with you makes can make the difference in creating a willingness to continue.

For some, this work will not just feel challenging—it may feel deeply personal. If this journey connects to:

> - lived experiences
> - personal pain
> - ongoing realities

Please know you are not expected to carry that weight alone. Take what you need from this work, step back when necessary, and seek support when needed.

This process is meant to **honor your humanity**, not overwhelm it. This work was not created to expose you. It was created to **walk with you**.

To guide, not force.
To invite, not demand.
To support, not overwhelm.

As part of the thought process in creating this "7 Series" platform, there is room for:

- ➢ Your questions
- ➢ Your pace
- ➢ Your process

You may not feel ready. You may not feel confident. You may not feel certain. And still, you can continue.

Take the next step. Stay present. Remain open. It is not easy work, but it is worthy.

A House Built Uneven: Race, Power, and the American Church

There is a story the American church has long preferred to tell about itself. It is a story of revival, conviction, evangelism, sacrifice, mission, and moral courage. It is a story populated by preachers, prayer meetings, camp meetings, hymnals, missionaries, altar calls, baptisms, and sanctuary testimonies. It is a story many Christians know by heart. It is also, in many cases, a selective story.

Beneath that familiar telling is another story, one that is not separate from the first but bound tightly to it. It is the story of how the church in America was formed within a racial order, adapted to it, benefited from it, defended it, suffered under it, and still bears its marks. It is the story of how one faith came to be practiced in profoundly unequal ways. It is the story of how the church proclaimed one gospel while inhabiting two moral worlds: one in which white Christians largely possessed the power to define theology, structure, leadership, and belonging, and another in which Black Christians and other Christians of color had to fight for spiritual dignity inside a system that often denied their full humanity.

To speak honestly about racial healing and reconciliation in the church, we must begin with a truth that is often softened in the name of civility: the racial divide in American Christianity was not created equally. It was not a mutual misunderstanding. It was not simply an unfortunate cultural drift. It was built inside a society where white dominance shaped law, wealth, education, space, power, and the church itself.

The segregation of the church did not arise because Black and white Christians equally desired separate religious lives. It arose because white-controlled structures determined who was welcomed, who was constrained, who was trusted, who was ordained, who was educated, who was funded, and whose version of Christian life would be treated as normal.

That truth matters because reconciliation built on vague language will always be shallow. When the story is made symmetrical, responsibility disappears. When responsibility disappears, repentance becomes abstract. And when repentance becomes abstract, institutions remain unchanged while everyone speaks the language of healing.

A faith-based course on racial healing and reconciliation must refuse that pattern. It must tell the truth with clarity, moral seriousness, and spiritual courage.

This reader is shaped around "The 7 Rhythms" of:

1. Personal Awareness,
2. Social Awareness,
3. Historical Awareness,
4. Religious Awareness,
5. Religious Responsibility,
6. Acceptance, and
7. Growth and Commitment.

These rhythms are not merely topics. They are movements of formation. They guide a person, a congregation, or a community from unexamined inheritance toward honest witness.

They ask not only:

➢ What happened, but
➢ What has happened to us because it happened.

They ask not only:

- ➤ What the church has believed, but
- ➤ How the church has been shaped by what it refused to confront.

And they insist that healing is not a sentiment. It is a disciplined, truth-telling, spiritually grounded practice.

Rhythm 1 - Personal Awareness: What has shaped me?

Every journey toward racial healing begins with a disruption. Something interrupts what once felt normal. A person hears a story they have never heard, notices a pattern they have not named, feels dissonance where they once felt ease, or realizes that what seemed universal was, in fact, particular. Personal awareness begins there, in the unsettling recognition that one's perspective was never neutral.

Many white Christians have grown up in churches where race could remain unnamed for years. They may have been taught to think of themselves simply as Christians, not as racialized Christians. Their worship may have felt standard, their theology objective, their church structure practical, their preaching style biblical, and their leadership patterns natural. Yet what felt natural was not without history. It was a particular cultural formation so centered that it did not need to identify itself. White church culture in America often enjoyed the privilege of appearing unmarked. It could call itself simply the church.

For many Black Christians, that option did not exist. Race was not theoretical. It was part of the experience of entering, serving, or even being measured by church spaces. It shaped whether one's preaching was seen as too emotional, whether one's music was seen as too expressive, whether one's grief over racial violence was seen as pastoral or divisive, and whether one's theology of justice was seen as faithful or political. Black Christians often had to know, from the beginning, that "church" was not experienced the same way by everyone.

This unevenness in awareness matters.

> ➢ One group has often had the option of racial silence; the other has often had to interpret that silence.
> ➢ One group could imagine race as occasional; the other often knew it as ongoing.
> ➢ One group could misunderstand segregation as preference; the other often knew it as inheritance, injury, and adaptation.

The first work, then, is not accusation but examination.

Personal awareness asks each participant to consider the sources of their formation.

> ➢ What stories about race were present in the home?
> ➢ What jokes were tolerated?
> ➢ What fears were normalized?

> What neighborhoods were considered good?
> What schools were described as safe?
> What kinds of worship were called reverent?
> What kinds of preaching were described as sound?
> What kinds of anger were accepted as leadership, and what kinds were dismissed as threatening?
> What national events entered church prayer, and which ones were ignored?
> What suffering counted as pastoral concern, and what suffering was categorized as political noise?

These are not peripheral questions. They are the spiritual archaeology of racial formation.

A church member may sincerely say, "I was never taught to hate anyone."

That may be true in a narrow sense. But personal awareness asks a deeper question: What were you taught to normalize? Because racial formation does not depend only on explicit hatred. It is also transmitted through proximity, distance, silence, assumption, avoidance, hierarchy, and habit. It can be communicated in what a church celebrates, whom it trusts, whom it hires, whom it comforts, and whom it expects to adjust.

A white Christian who has spent decades in church may discover, often with sincere surprise, that race was absent from discipleship not because it was unimportant, but because the church spaces he inhabited were already aligned with his social location. He or she did not have to learn how race worked because the structure was working in his or her favor.

A Black Christian may discover that what is interpreted merely as spiritual loneliness was also structural isolation.

A Latino Christian may realize that inclusion in attendance never translated into influence in decision-making.

 An Asian American Christian may recognize that being welcomed as long as one remains non-disruptive is not the same thing as being fully seen.

Personal awareness is difficult because it destabilizes innocence. It does not necessarily tell a person they intended harm. It tells them something harder: that they may have been well-intentioned yet profoundly shaped by patterns they neither chose, noticed, nor challenged. The goal is not shame. The goal is truthfulness. Shame often collapses inward, becoming self-protection. Truthfulness opens outward, becoming the beginning of transformation.

Questions for Reflection

1. When did race first become visible to you in your faith experience?

2. What did your church teach about race directly, and what did it teach indirectly through silence?

3. What worship practices, leadership styles, or theological emphases did you absorb as normal?

4. Whose experiences were centered in your faith formation, and whose were missing?

5. What are you beginning to see now that you did not have language for before?

Rhythm 2 - Social Awareness:

Personal awareness naturally leads to social awareness, because no one is formed in isolation. Individual beliefs are cultivated within larger arrangements of power. Churches do not hover above history as purely spiritual communities. They are situated in neighborhoods, funded by economic patterns, supplied by institutions, and carried along by cultural assumptions. They are social bodies as well as spiritual ones.

The American church was built inside a nation whose racial order influenced land ownership, education, law, wealth accumulation, political representation, and mobility.

These forces shaped who could build church buildings, who could access seminaries, who could travel for ministry, who could publish, who could lead denominations, who could network, and who could imagine themselves as the face of Christian authority. White Christians did not simply happen to occupy positions of leadership; they occupied them in a nation that systematically advantaged them in the accumulation of institutional power.

That power was not confined to overt racism or malicious intent. It settled into systems. Seminaries admitted some and excluded others. Boards trusted certain resumes and discounted others. Search committees used terms like maturity, fit, polish, and credibility in ways that reflected racialized norms. Donors favored continuity. Congregations equated familiarity with soundness, and networks reproduced themselves. Churches that called themselves Bible-believing often mistook cultural comfort for spiritual discernment.

This is how systems work. They do not always require declared hostility. They operate through habit, procedure, expectation, and inherited design.

> A church may honestly say, "We do not discriminate," and still repeatedly elevate white leadership because the mechanisms by which leadership is recognized were built within white-centered environments.

> A church may describe its worship as open to all while centering a style, cadence, and aesthetic that signal whose comfort is primary.

> A denomination may celebrate diversity while requiring candidates

to assimilate to dominant cultural expectations to advance.

Social awareness is the movement from seeing racism only as personal prejudice to seeing racialized inequality as embedded structure. It recognizes that churches mirror housing segregation, educational inequality, and neighborhood history.

If a church sits in a suburb shaped by white flight, that matters.

If its wealth was accumulated during periods when Black families were excluded from mortgages or neighborhoods, that matters.

If its current leadership pipeline depends on institutions that have historically been inaccessible to many communities of color, that matters.

These matters are not distractions from the gospel. They are part of telling the truth about the conditions in which the gospel has been proclaimed.

Consider a multiracial church with a visibly diverse congregation. The music team includes people of several backgrounds. The website uses the language of belonging. The stage occasionally includes voices of color. Yet the senior leadership team remains overwhelmingly white. The elders remain overwhelmingly white. The preaching voice remains overwhelmingly white. Financial decisions are made by overwhelmingly white bodies. Conflict is resolved according to overwhelmingly white norms of communication. The church calls itself diverse, but the center of gravity does not move. Diversity becomes presentational rather than structural.

This is a common scenario because many congregations confuse

representation with redistribution. They imagine that inviting people into a preexisting structure is the same thing as sharing power. It is not. True social awareness asks who built the table, who sets the agenda, who interprets the conflict, who defines unity, and who pays the cost of belonging.

It also asks how churches understand neutrality. Often what is called neutrality is merely the protection of the dominant arrangement.

 A church may decline to address racialized suffering on the grounds that it wants to avoid politics. But that restraint often falls unevenly. It does not suspend all cultural commitments. It simply preserves the ones already normalized. **Silence can function as a social decision in favor of the existing order.**

The work here is not only to identify bad actors. It is to examine inherited systems.

A congregation serious about healing
must ask how its structures were formed,
whom they protect, whom they burden,
and what they would require of others to
belong.

Questions for Reflection:

1. What social systems shaped the church you know best: neighborhood patterns, educational access, wealth, or denominational history?

2. Who usually gets recognized as leader material in your church, and why?

3. What unspoken expectations shape who is heard, trusted, and promoted?

4. Where has your church confused diversity in attendance with equity in power?

5. What would change if your congregation examined its systems instead of only its intentions?

Rhythm 3 - Historical Awareness: What happened, and how is it still with us?

Historical awareness is the refusal to let the past become vague. It resists the comforting habit of describing racial injury in general terms without naming the church's concrete participation in it. The American church did not merely live through slavery, segregation, and racial terror as a bystander. Large portions of it provided moral cover, theological argument, institutional reinforcement, or practical silence.

This is one of the central truths any faithful racial healing process must hold firmly: many white Christian leaders and institutions in America defended slavery not despite their theology, but through it.

- ➤ They searched scripture for sanction, emphasized obedience over liberation, and formed interpretations that aligned Christian duty with racial hierarchy.
- ➤ They trained consciences to adapt to injustice.
- ➤ They did not merely fail to oppose evil strongly enough. Many actively gave evil religious grammar.

This matters because it reveals that distorted theology was not a side error. It was part of institutional Christian formation. Churches taught people how to see racial order as morally acceptable.

They shaped imaginations, not only laws. They helped create the conditions in which white Christians could participate in or benefit from racial domination while preserving a sense of righteousness.

Black Christians responded to this contradiction not with passive acceptance, but with spiritual creativity, resilience, and resistance. They encountered the same Bible and heard in it a radically different word. Where white-controlled Christianity often emphasized compliance, Black Christians heard Exodus. Where white pulpits often spiritualized suffering, Black Christians heard the prophets cry out against injustice. Where dominant institutions stressed order, Black Christians found a Savior acquainted with grief and oppression. Out of exclusion and spiritual theft, the Black church emerged as a space of dignity, leadership, refuge, truth-telling, and communal survival.

It is crucial to name this accurately. The Black church was not the mirror-image equivalent of white segregation. It was not the equal-and-opposite choice. It arose under pressure. It was forged as a response to white exclusion, white violence, white control, and white theological dominance. It became not only a worshiping community but a moral and communal infrastructure in a nation that routinely denied Black humanity. To flatten this history into "people preferred to worship separately" is to erase both coercion and courage.

As the nation moved from slavery into Reconstruction, Jim Crow, and the long age of segregation, churches continued to reflect and reinforce racial hierarchy.

- ➢ Denominations split along race-related lines.
- ➢ Congregations institutionalized separation.
- ➢ Leadership remained racially bounded.
- ➢ Theological education remained unevenly accessible.
- ➢ White Christian institutions kept authority.

> ➤ Black churches developed parallel systems because they had to.

The church was not accidentally segregated. It was organized that way.

The civil rights era did not create racial tension in the church; it exposed the church's loyalties. Black churches became centers of movement, life, strategy, hope, protest, and moral witness. Many white churches remained silent, hesitant, hostile, or committed to an order they called peace. This divergence matters. It shows that the question was never simply whether Christians believed in love. It was a question of whether love had enough moral substance to confront power.

Historical awareness rejects the phrase "that was then" as a way of trivializing continuity. The past is not gone simply because the law changed. The institutions built during periods of exclusion often persist, carrying forward patterns of wealth, legitimacy, leadership, and memory.

> ➤ A church building may be renamed, but its donor culture may remain.
> ➤ A denomination may issue a statement of apology, but its pipeline may still privilege those shaped by the old center.
> ➤ A congregation may proudly affirm diversity while remaining ignorant of how its own founding was intertwined with segregation, exclusion, or white flight.

Truth-telling in this rhythm requires specificity. It may require churches to research their own history.

> ➤ Who founded the congregation?
> ➤ Where did its first members come from?
> ➤ What racial patterns shaped its neighborhood?

- ➢ How did it respond to school integration, housing change, busing, civil rights legislation, or public racial crises?
- ➢ Did the church open its leadership equally?
- ➢ Did it remain silent while others suffered?
- ➢ Did it benefit from patterns of exclusion even without naming them?

Many congregations do not know, and that ignorance itself is revealing. It suggests that historical ignorance has functioned as a luxury. For those harmed by history, memory was survival. For those advantaged by history, forgetting was often comfort.

Questions for Reflection

1. What parts of your church's history have been told, and what parts have not?

2. How did white dominance shape the church in America structurally, not just relationally?

3. How does the emergence of the Black church challenge false ideas of symmetrical separation?

4. What historical realities does your congregation still benefit from without naming?

5. What would it mean for your church to tell its own story truthfully?

Rhythm 4 - Religious Awareness: How has theology itself been shaped by racialized culture?

Religious awareness asks a question many churches resist because it sounds too disruptive: **What if the church's theology has been shaped, constrained, or distorted by the culture in which it was formed?** Not whether the Bible changes, but whether our interpretations, emphases, instincts, and applications have been culturally conditioned in ways we have mistaken for timeless truth.

White American Christianity often centered on themes that aligned with social stability: personal salvation, individual morality, spiritual order, self-discipline, respectability, and obedience. These are not illegitimate biblical themes, and the problem is not that they exist. The problem, presented as a question, is: what happened when they were elevated while justice, liberation, communal repair, prophetic protest, and structural sin were minimized or treated as secondary?

This imbalance did not happen by accident. In a society structured by racial inequality, it was more convenient for dominant religious institutions to stress the sins of the heart than the sins embedded in social order.

> ➢ It was more comfortable to address personal behavior than racial capitalism, segregation, or exclusion.
> ➢ It was safer to preach patience to the oppressed than repentance to the powerful.

> It was easier to spiritualize unity than to practice it by relinquishing control.

Black Christian traditions, by contrast, often developed theological sensibilities shaped by suffering, endurance, communal hope, and divine justice. This did not mean Black Christians cared less about personal transformation. It meant they could not afford a theology disconnected from concrete liberation. The God they encountered was not merely the manager of private piety. God was the sustainer of a people, the judge of unjust systems, the hearer of cries, and the giver of dignity in a world designed to deny it.

Religious awareness, then, does not ask people to choose between personal faith and social truth.

- ➢ It asks them to recognize that the dominant forms of theology in America have often reflected white social location while presenting themselves as universally objective.
- ➢ It asks whether a church's idea of unity requires people of color to mute parts of their reality to preserve comfort.
- ➢ It asks whether calls for reconciliation have functioned as a shortcut around justice.
- ➢ It asks whether statements like "preach the gospel, not politics" have served to narrow the gospel until it no longer disrupts racialized power.

Many churches become anxious here because they fear that naming the cultural dimensions of theology will undermine biblical authority. But the opposite can be true.

Honest religious awareness can protect the church from mistaking its habits for holiness. It can expose where culture was baptized and called doctrine. It can uncover how power influenced whose commentaries were trusted, whose testimonies were centered, and whose lived experiences were treated as spiritually instructive.

This is especially important in integrated or multiracial churches. A congregation may welcome multiple racial groups while maintaining a single dominant theological and cultural lens. It may sing one song from another tradition while preserving a whole framework of leadership, time, decision-making, emotional expression, conflict resolution, and pastoral emphasis that remains centered in white Protestant norms. The church may call itself broad because it borrowed symbols, while its deeper structures remain unchallenged.

Religious awareness moves beyond symbolic diversity. It asks whether the church is prepared to let marginalized experience teach it something about the character of God, the meaning of discipleship, the nature of sin, and the practice of justice. It asks whether the people who have suffered most under racial distortion might also have the clearest testimony about what redemption requires.

1. What themes has your church emphasized most consistently, and why?

2. What biblical themes related to justice, lament, liberation, or communal repair have been neglected?

3. Where might your church be confusing cultural norms with theological truth?

4. How has race shaped which voices and interpretations are considered most authoritative?

5. What might your understanding of Christian faith look like if formed

from the underside of history rather than the center of power?

Rhythm 5 - Religious Responsibility:

What does faith require now?

By the time a person or congregation reaches this rhythm, the question is no longer whether racial distortion exists. The question is what faithfulness requires in response.

Religious responsibility is the movement from awareness to moral action. It refuses the temptation to admire truth without obeying it.

Churches are often willing to acknowledge pain in general language; however, seemingly less willing to change the arrangements that reproduce it. A congregation may host a panel discussion, preach a sermon, issue a statement, or observe a special service following a public racial crisis. These gestures can matter. But when they are not connected to structural examination and concrete change, they become liturgies of self-protection. They allow the church to appear responsive without becoming accountable.

Religious responsibility asks harder questions.

> ➢ If a church now knows that its leadership patterns reflect inherited inequity, what will it do?
> ➢ If it knows that its worship culture centers one group's comfort, what will it do?
> ➢ If it knows that its silence on racial suffering has communicated indifference, what will it do?
> ➢ If it knows that its discipleship model has not prepared people to understand racial history, what will it do?

This rhythm is where many communities stall. They mistake emotional agreement for transformation. People say, "That was powerful," or "I never saw it that way before," and then return to the same structures, the same committees, the same assumptions, the same hiring practices, the same defensiveness when change threatens familiarity. Insight becomes an event rather than practice.

Responsibility means choosing disruption. It may mean changing who teaches and preaches. It may mean revising leadership pathways. It may mean auditing church history, partnerships, investments, and curriculum. It may mean redistributing influence. It may mean funding initiatives led by those who have historically been sidelined. It may mean sustained training, not one-time inspiration. It may mean that some people lose the comfort of always setting the tone.

That is precisely why responsibility is spiritual work. It tests whether the church loves reconciliation as an idea or as a cost-bearing calling.

White-led churches, in particular, must resist the urge to frame responsibility only as interpersonal kindness. Personal warmth matters, but it is insufficient. A church can be friendly and still unequal. It can be welcoming and still center white assumptions. It can publicly denounce racism and still operate in ways that protect racialized power. Responsibility requires institutions to do what individuals alone cannot: change the conditions that shape the community.

It also requires a new understanding of repentance. Repentance is not merely feeling bad about wrong. It is turning. In congregational life, turning means altering pattern, structure, and imagination. A church that says it laments segregation but never examines its own concentrated power has not yet repented. A church that values diverse attendance but refuses shared authority has not yet repented. A church that invokes unity whenever critique arises may actually be using spiritual language to avoid repentance.

Religious responsibility is not punitive. It is restorative. It is the work of bringing the church's life into greater alignment with its confession. But restoration without honesty is fiction. Responsibility insists that faith become embodied in the architecture of community life.

Questions for Reflection

1. What does repentance look like for a church, not just for an individual?

2. Where has your congregation chosen harmony over honesty or comfort over justice?

3. What concrete structures would need to change for your church's values to become visible?

4. How is power shared in your church now, and how might it be shared differently?

5. What risks is your church willing to take in order to become more truthful and just?

Rhythm 6 - Acceptance:

Can we stay present long enough for the truth to work on us?

Acceptance is often misunderstood. It does not mean approving every painful fact or resigning oneself to guilt. It means refusing to deny. It means learning how to remain in the presence of truth without rushing to defend oneself, diluting reality, changing the subject, or demanding immediate comfort.

This is one of the most difficult rhythms because the truth about race in the church almost always provokes emotion.

> ➢ Some feel grief.
> ➢ Some feel anger.
> ➢ Some feel shame.
> ➢ Some feel exposed.
> ➢ Some feel vindicated.

- ➢ Some feel exhausted because none of this is new to them.
- ➢ Some feel accused even when no personal accusation has been made.
- ➢ Some feel the instinct to say, "But not all," "That is not my experience," or "This is too divisive."

Acceptance asks a different posture. Instead of responding first with self-exoneration, it invites listening. Instead of trying to determine whether one is personally guilty enough to keep paying attention, it asks whether the truth being told is real and worthy of moral response. It asks people to notice how quickly they move to protect their self-image. It asks congregations to notice how quickly they label discomfort as disunity.

This rhythm is essential because this is where many churches abort the healing process. They can handle general calls to love. They can even handle selective historical facts. But when the implications begin to touch leadership, memory, theology, or present structure, resistance rises. People become impatient. They say the church should move on. They ask when the conversation will end. They complain that the focus on race is becoming excessive. In doing so, they reveal that they may have wanted inspiration without transformation.

Acceptance does not mean endless analysis without movement. It means allowing the truth to do its work before rushing to control it. **It means understanding that communities harmed over generations cannot be asked to trust overnight.** It means acknowledging that those long centered may experience equality as loss because they are unfamiliar with decentering. It means understanding that lament is not a threat to unity, but one of its necessary preconditions.

This is also where pastoral care must deepen. A healing process that tells hard truths without making room for grief, fear, and honest struggle can become brittle. But a process that prioritizes emotional reassurance over truth becomes dishonest. Acceptance holds both: the demand for truth and the patience to remain with people as they are changed by it.

For white Christians, acceptance may require surrendering the need to be seen as innocent before being willing to be transformed. For Christians of color, acceptance may require deciding whether and how to remain engaged without allowing the process to become another site of extraction or erasure. For churches as institutions, acceptance may require admitting that the image they

prefer to hold of themselves is
incomplete.

Only what is faced can be healed.
Acceptance is the practice of facing.

Questions for Reflection

1. What truths in this journey are hardest for you to sit with?

2. How do you usually respond when your understanding of the church is challenged?

3. What defenses arise in you when power, leadership, or white dominance are named directly?

4. Where might your desire for comfort be interrupting the work of truth?

5. What would it mean for your church to stay in the process without rushing to closure?

Rhythm 7 - Growth and Commitment: What kind of church are we becoming?

The final rhythm is not a conclusion so much as a covenant. Growth and Commitment ask whether the church will translate truth into enduring practice.

Many communities begin with energy and sincerity. Fewer remain when the work becomes slow, structural, and costly. **Yet this is precisely where reconciliation becomes real: not in the moment of awakening, but in the long discipline of becoming different.**

Growth means more than increasing awareness. It means reshaping communal life. It means that leadership pathways, preaching patterns, discipleship structures, hiring processes, partnership decisions, resource allocations, and definitions of maturity all come under examination. It means that the church no longer assumes that good intentions are enough. It begins asking whether its actual life reflects the body it proclaims.

Commitment is tested by time. A congregation may be moved by a powerful season of learning, but what happens one year later?

- ➢ Have the names on the decision-making bodies changed?
- ➢ Has the church built sustained relationships with Black-led and other historically marginalized ministries without instrumentalizing them?
- ➢ Has the curriculum changed?
- ➢ Has the pulpit widened?
- ➢ Has the budget revealed priorities?
- ➢ Has the church learned to respond to public racial suffering with moral

clarity rather than anxious neutrality?

> ➤ Has it developed practices of accountability?

The future of racial healing in the church will not be secured by sentiment alone. It will be secured by habits.

> ➤ Habits of shared leadership.
> ➤ Habits of honest teaching.
> ➤ Habits of lament.
> ➤ Habits of interruption when harmful assumptions arise.
> ➤ Habits of asking who is centered and who is paying the cost.
> ➤ Habits of measuring not only attendance but belonging, not only diversity but equity, not only peace but justice.

Growth also requires imagination. Many churches are trapped because they can only picture two options: either remain as they are or descend into endless conflict.

They need a third vision. A church can become more truthful, more just, more shared, more representative, and more spiritually credible. It can become a place where diversity is not ornamental, where Black presence is not welcomed only on dominant terms, where leadership does not default to whiteness, where theology is deep enough to name structural sin, and where reconciliation is not confused with silence.

This does not mean erasing distinct traditions or dissolving the Black church into a colorblind ideal. That would repeat the violence of false universality. The goal is not sameness. The goal is truth, dignity, justice, mutuality, and shared witness.

 The Black church remains a historic, theological, and communal gift precisely because it was forged in resistance to white distortion. Racial healing does not require its disappearance. It requires the end of the structures that made such separate refuge necessary.

Commitment means accepting that this work will outlast any single workshop, sermon series, or document. It is generational. But that is not a reason for delay. It is a reason for seriousness. The church is always forming someone. The question is what kind of people, what kind of community, and what kind of witness it is producing now.

Questions for Reflection

1. What specific commitments will your church make in the next year, not just in theory but in structure?

2. How will you know whether change is actually happening?

3. Whose voices need greater authority in shaping the future of your congregation?

4. What habits will help your church stay in this work when enthusiasm fades?

5. What kind of witness do you want your church to offer the world in the years ahead?

Real Church Scenarios

Scenario 1: The Diverse Room, the White Center

A church in a growing suburb has become visibly diverse over the last decade. The congregation includes white, Black, Latino, and Asian members. The church website highlights this diversity as a sign of the gospel. Yet the senior pastor, executive team, elder board, and most department heads are white.

Sermons on race are rare. Music occasionally includes cultural variety, but church conflict is interpreted almost entirely through dominant cultural assumptions.

Members of color feel welcomed but not weight-bearing.

The church believes it is already doing well because attendance looks different from what it used to be.

Questions:

1. What is the difference between representation and shared power here?

2. What signals might members of color be receiving even if no one says exclusionary things aloud?

3. What concrete next steps would move this church beyond diversity language into structural equity?

Scenario 2: The Founder's Legacy

An older church discovers that its celebrated founding pastor publicly supported segregation in the 1950's and opposed civil rights protests in its city. A building on campus still bears his name.

 Some members argue that reopening the issue is divisive and disrespectful to church history. Others insist that a truthful reckoning is necessary if the church wants credibility in its reconciliation efforts.

1. What does faithfulness require when cherished institutional memory conflicts with moral truth?

2. How can a church distinguish honoring history from sanitizing it?

3. What would repentance look like in this case?

Scenario 3: The Search Committee

A church seeking a new senior pastor says it wants the best person for the role. It receives applications from several gifted candidates, including Black and Latino pastors with strong records of preaching and leadership.

 During the process, committee members repeatedly describe one white candidate as the strongest cultural fit. When pressed, they mention his communication style, polish, and ease with the congregation.

They do not recognize how their language reflects preexisting expectations about authority.

Questions:

1. How does racialized normativity operate in this scenario?

2. What would a more honest and equitable search process require

3. How might a congregation need to be formed differently before such a process begins?

Scenario 4: The Public Crisis

After a nationally visible incident of racial violence, younger members ask their church to pray publicly, preach clearly, and host a conversation about racial grief and justice.

Church leaders hesitate, saying they do not want to politicize the pulpit.

Several members of color interpret the silence as abandonment. Some leave quietly over the next year.

Questions:

1. What message does the church's silence communicate?

2. How is neutrality functioning in this case?

3. What does pastoral care require when public suffering falls unevenly across a congregation?

Scenario 5: The One-Time Initiative

A church launches a reconciliation task force after a period of internal pressure. It hosts three events, issues a statement, and then allows the initiative to fade when attendance declines and resistance emerge.

Leaders privately conclude that the church is not ready. The members who needed the church most to stay engaged interpret the retreat as predictable.

1. Why do so many churches stop at symbolic action?

2. What would it mean to treat racial healing as core discipleship rather than a temporary initiative?

3. How can accountability be built so the work survives discomfort?

Closing Narrative

The church in America has often wanted reconciliation without reckoning. It has wanted unity without truth, diversity without redistribution, and healing without confession. But the gospel is not that thin. It does not permit reconciliation to become a slogan used to bypass responsibility. It does not sanctify peace that depends on silence. It does not ask the wounded to carry the burden of everyone else's comfort.

A faithful church must become more honest than that.

It must become a church that can say plainly that white dominance shaped the American church historically and continues to influence it now. It must become a church that can distinguish the existence of the Black church as a sacred and necessary response from the white-controlled structures that made such refuge necessary. It must become a church that no longer treats its own habits as universal, its own comfort as neutral, or its own memory as complete.

And it must become a church willing to be changed.

That change will not happen because the church learns better language alone. It will happen because communities decide that truth matters more than image, justice matters more than comfort, and shared power matters more than preserved control. It will happen because pastors preach more courageously, leaders listen more honestly, congregations study their histories more deeply, and Christians allow the Spirit to confront not only their private sin but their public arrangements.

The credibility of the church's witness depends on this. Not because the church must be perfect before it can speak, but because it cannot proclaim a reconciling Christ while protecting unreconciled structures without damaging the very message it carries.

This is why a Christian, faith-based racial healing and reconciliation course is necessary. It is not an accessory to discipleship. It is part of discipleship. It is not about importing a foreign agenda into the church. It is about confronting the church's own history, habits, and witness in the light of the gospel it claims to preach.

The question before the church is no longer whether race has shaped it. The question is whether it loves Christ, truth, and neighbor enough to let that shaping be undone and remade.

That is the work.

That is the calling.

That is the hope.

Scripture & Historical References

Scripture references, where applicable, are drawn from widely accepted biblical translations. Historical and statistical references are based on publicly available research, including but not limited to:

Pew Research Center

National Congregations Study / Baylor University

Christianity Today

Good Faith Media

Statistical Inserts and Data Callouts

Data Callout 1

About two-thirds of U.S. churchgoers say they attend congregations where most people are the same race as they are. This underscores how racial sameness remains the default experience of church life for many Christians.

Data Callout 2

Pew has reported that roughly two-thirds of congregations have leaders of the same race as the congregation's majority, indicating that congregational composition and leadership identity remain tightly linked.

Data Callout 3

Research on multiracial congregations has shown growth over recent decades, but these churches still represent a minority of U.S. congregations rather than the norm.

Data Callout 4

Studies of multiracial megachurches have found that senior leadership remains disproportionately white, even when the congregations themselves are racially diverse.

Data Callout 5

Historical research consistently shows that American congregations have long mirrored broader racial segregation patterns in society rather than serving as a strong counterexample to them.

Indexed Source List

- [1] Pew Research Center, "Race and Ethnicity in Religious Congregations," February 26, 2025.

- [2] Baylor University reporting on racially diverse congregations in the United States.

- [3] National Congregations Study and related reporting on multiracial church growth.

- [4] Reporting on racial makeup of leadership in multiracial megachurches.

- [5] Historical scholarship on segregation in American congregations.

Bibliography

Alexander, Michelle. *The New Jim Crow: Mass Incarceration in the Age of Colorblindness*. New York: The New Press, 2010.

Anderson, Allan. *An Introduction to Pentecostalism: Global Charismatic Christianity.* Cambridge: Cambridge University Press, 2014.

Baldwin, James. *The Fire Next Time*. New York: Vintage International, 1963.

Barna Group. *The State of the Church 2024*. Ventura, CA: Barna Group, 2024.

Bonhoeffer, Dietrich. *Life Together*. New York: HarperOne, 1954.

Bracey, Christopher A. *Saviors or Sellouts: The Promise and Peril of Black Conservatism*. Boston: Beacon Press, 2008.

Butler, Anthea. *White Evangelical Racism: The Politics of Morality in America*. Chapel Hill: University of North Carolina Press, 2021.

Cone, James H. *A Black Theology of Liberation*. Maryknoll, NY: Orbis Books, 1970.

Cone, James H. *The Cross and the Lynching Tree*. Maryknoll, NY: Orbis Books, 2011.

DeYoung, Curtiss Paul, et al. *United by Faith: The Multiracial Congregation as an Answer to the Problem of Race*. New York: Oxford University Press, 2003.

Du Bois, W.E.B. *The Souls of Black Folk*. Chicago: A.C. McClurg & Co., 1903.

Edwards, Jonathan. *The Works of Jonathan Edwards. Various editions.*

Emerson, Michael O., and Christian Smith. *Divided by Faith: Evangelical Religion and the Problem of Race in*

America. New York: Oxford University Press, 2000.

Feagin, Joe R. *The White Racial Frame: Centuries of Racial Framing and Counter-Framing*. New York: Routledge, 2013.

Glaude Jr., Eddie S. *Begin Again: James Baldwin's America and Its Urgent Lessons for Our Own*. New York: Crown, 2020.

Harvey, Paul. *Freedom's Coming: Religious Culture and the Shaping of the South from the Civil War through the Civil Rights Era*. Chapel Hill: University of North Carolina Press, 2005.

Hunt, Teri. *Black Religious Life in the United States*. New York: Oxford University Press, 2018.

King Jr., Martin Luther. *Why We Can't Wait*. New York: Harper & Row, 1964.

King Jr., Martin Luther. *Strength to Love*. Philadelphia: Fortress Press, 1963.

McNeil, Brenda Salter. *Roadmap to Reconciliation 2.0: Moving Communities into Unity, Wholeness and Justice.* Downers Grove, IL: InterVarsity Press, 2020.

Perkins, John M. *Let Justice Roll Down.* Ventura, CA: Regal Books, 2006.

Pew Research Center. *Race and Ethnicity in U.S. Religious Congregations.* Washington, DC: Pew Research Center, 2025.

Rah, Soong-Chan. *The Next Evangelicalism: Freeing the Church from Western Cultural Captivity.* Downers Grove, IL: InterVarsity Press, 2009.

Tisby, Jemar. *The Color of Compromise: The Truth about the American Church's Complicity in Racism.* Grand Rapids, MI: Zondervan, 2019.

Tisby, Jemar. *How to Fight Racism: Courageous Christianity and the Journey*

Toward Racial Justice. Grand Rapids, MI: Zondervan, 2021.

Williams, Daniel K. *God's Own Party: The Making of the Christian Right*. New York: Oxford University Press, 2010.

Woodson, Carter G. *The Mis-Education of the Negro*. Washington, DC: Associated Publishers, 1933.

Recommended Reading

The work of racial healing and reconciliation does not end with this reader. For those who desire to go deeper—historically, spiritually, and practically—the following resources provide insight, challenge, and guidance. These works have shaped the conversation and continue to inform the journey toward truth and transformation within the church.

Understanding History

Jemar Tisby
The Color of Compromise
A clear and sobering account of how the American church has historically participated in and sustained racial division.

W.E.B. Du Bois
The Souls of Black Folk
A foundational work that offers insight into the lived experience of Black Americans and the role of religion in shaping identity and resistance.

Carter G. Woodson
The Mis-Education of the Negro
A critical examination of how systems shape thought, identity, and perception—relevant to both society and church life.

Understanding Church and Race

Michael O. Emerson & Christian Smith
Divided by Faith
A sociological analysis explaining why racial division persists within American evangelical churches.

Curtiss Paul DeYoung et al.
United by Faith
A look at multiracial congregations and both the promise and challenges they represent.

Soong-Chan Rah
The Next Evangelicalism
A compelling critique of Western cultural dominance within the church and a call toward a more holistic expression of faith.

Theological Reflection and Challenge

James H. Cone

The Cross and the Lynching Tree

A profound theological reflection connecting the suffering of Christ with the historical reality of racial violence in America.

John M. Perkins

Let Justice Roll Down

A foundational voice in Christian reconciliation, emphasizing justice, community, and lived faith.

Brenda Salter McNeil

Roadmap to Reconciliation 2.0

A practical and spiritual framework for moving communities toward unity, justice, and restoration.

Contemporary Cultural Awareness

Michelle Alexander

The New Jim Crow

An examination of systemic inequality in modern America and its lasting impact on communities.

Anthea Butler

White Evangelical Racism

A critical exploration of how race and politics

have shaped white evangelical identity and influence.

Eddie S. Glaude Jr.
Begin Again
A reflective and urgent call to confront America's racial history and imagine a different future.

For Personal Reflection

Dietrich Bonhoeffer
Life Together
A classic exploration of Christian community, challenging readers to consider what authentic shared life truly requires.

Martin Luther King Jr.
Strength to Love
Sermons that connect faith, justice, and moral courage in a way that remains deeply relevant today.

9 798994 627457